Galactic Mission

Story by Richard Platt

LONDON, NEW YORK, MUNICH,
MELBOURNE, and DELHI

DK LONDON
Series Editor Deborah Lock
US Senior Editor Shannon Beatty
Assistant Editor Katy Lennon
Producers, Pre-production
Francesca Wardell, Vikki Nousiainen

DK DELHI
Editor Nandini Gupta
Assistant Art Editor Tanvi Nathyal
DTP Designers Anita Yadav, Vijay Kandwal
Picture Researcher Surya Sarangi
Deputy Managing Editor Soma B. Chowdhury

Reading Consultant
Dr. Linda Gambrell, Ph.D.

First American Edition, 2014

Published in the United States by
DK Publishing
345 Hudson Street, 4th Floor
New York, New York 10014

14 15 16 17 18 10 9 8 7 6 5 4 3 2 1
001—256560—July/14

Copyright © 2014 Dorling Kindersley Limited

All rights reserved.
Without limiting the rights under copyright reserved above, no part of this publication may be reproduced, stored in or
introduced into a retrieval system, or transmitted, in any form, or by any means (electronic, mechanical, photocopying,
recording, or otherwise), without the prior written permission of both the copyright owner and the above publisher of this book.

Published in Great Britain by Dorling Kindersley Limited.

A catalog record for this book is available from the Library of Congress.

ISBN: 978-1-4654-1977-4 (pb)
ISBN: 978-1-4654-1978-1 (hc)

Printed and bound in China by South China Printing Co., Ltd.

DK books are available at special discounts when purchased in bulk for sales promotions, premiums, fund-raising, or
educational use. For details, contact: DK Publishing Special Markets, 345 Hudson Street, 4th Floor, New York, New York
10014 or SpecialSales@dk.com.

The publisher would like to thank the following for their kind permission to reproduce their photographs:
(Key: a-above; b-below/bottom; c-center; f-far; l-left; r-right; t-top)

1 **Corbis:** Kevin Lafin / Stocktrek Images. 3–4 **Corbis:** Topic Photo Agency. 6–7 **Alamy Images:** Yoji Hirose / Galaxy Picture
Library. 8 **Dreamstime.com:** Danicek (br). 9 **Corbis:** Yuli Seperi / Demotix / Demotix (cra). 10 **Corbis:** Walter Myers /
Stocktrek Images (t). 10–116 **Dreamstime.com:** Ruslan Gilmanshin (b/Earth). 12–13 **Alamy Images:** Stephen Barnes / Law
and Order. 14 **Alamy Images:** Jason Langley. 17 **Alamy Images:** Bernhard Classen (b). 19 **Dreamstime.com:** Nikkytok (b).
21 **Corbis:** Andrzej Wojcicki / Science Photo Library. 24–123 **Corbis:** Mark Stevenson / Stocktrek Images (Background).
24 **Alamy Images:** Victor Habbick Visions / Science Photo Library (c). 25 **Alamy Images:** Victor Habbick Visions / Science
Photo Library (cr, clb, cl); Dennis Hallinan (cra, cla). **Fotolia:** Dundanim (bl). 26 **Dorling Kindersley:** Space
and Rocket Center, Alabama (cr). 27 **Alamy Images:** Eddie Toro (cr). **Fotolia:** Dundanim (t). 28 **Corbis:** Roger Ressmeyer (t).
29 **Corbis:** Andrzej Wojcicki / Science Photo Library (b). 31 **Alamy Images:** NASA Photo (t). 33 **Dreamstime.com:**
BenMcleish (b). 34 **Dreamstime.com:** Brett Critchley (t). 38–39 **Corbis:** Walter Myers / Stocktrek Images.
40 **Dreamstime.com:** Valeriya Smidt (tl). 42–43 **Dreamstime.com:** Augusto Cabral (t). 44 **Corbis:** Topic Photo Agency (t).
47 **Dreamstime.com:** Clearviewstock (b). 48 **Dreamstime.com:** Serge Horta (t). 50 **Dreamstime.com:** Carlos1967 (b).
52–53 **Getty Images:** George Frey. 54 **Alamy Images:** Radius Images (cra); Marc Tielemans (cl). **Getty Images:** John B.
Carnett / Popular Science (cr). 55 **Alamy Images:** Ruth Jenkinson / Science Photo Library (tr). **Dreamstime.com:** Monkey
Business Images (tl). 57 **Corbis:** Jon Hicks (c). 58 **Corbis:** Ron Sachs / CNP (t). 59 **Dreamstime.com:** Glenn Jenkinson (b).
61 **Alamy Images:** Fabian Schmidt (b). 65 **Dreamstime.com:** Alhovik (b). 68–69 **Corbis:** Walter Myers / Stocktrek
Images(Rockets). **Dreamstime.com:** Dimitar Marinov (Saturn). 70 **Dreamstime.com:** Jon Helgason (ca). 70–71 **Corbis:**
Walter Myers / Stocktrek Images (ca). 71 **Corbis:** NASA / Handout / CNP (bl); NASA / Handout (t); HO / Reuters (br).
72 **Getty Images:** Getty Images / Handout (clb). 72–73 **Getty Images:** NASA / Handout. 73 **Corbis:** Roger Ressmeyer (crb).
Getty Images: Time & Life Pictures (clb). 74 **Corbis:** Tomasz Dabrowski / Stocktrek Images (cl). 75 **Corbis:** Roger Ressmeyer (t).
77 **Dreamstime.com:** Dmitriy Karelin (b/Star); Tovovan (b/Monitor); Artur Marciniec (Background).
79 **Dreamstime.com:** Artur Marciniec (Background); Tovovan (t). 81 **Dreamstime.com:** Artur Marciniec (Background);
Tovovan (b). 84–85 **Pearson Asset Library:** Oxford Designers & Illustrators Ltd (c). 84 **Corbis:**
85 **Corbis:** NASA / JPL-Caltech (bl). 86 **Alamy Images:** Stocktrek Images, Inc. (cra). **Corbis:** NASA / JPLCaltech (b).
87 **Corbis:** Aaron Horowitz. 90 **Corbis:** Roger Ressmeyer (t). 95 **Dreamstime.com:** Stefanie Winkler (b/Space). 96 **Corbis:**
Andrzej Wojcicki / Science Photo Library (cb). 100–101 **Dreamstime.com:** Matthew Benoit. 102–103 **Alamy Images:** Paul Fleet.
104 **Alamy Images:** Moviestore collection Ltd (cr); Pictorial Press Ltd (c). **Corbis:** Bettmann (cl). 105 **Alamy Images:**
Moviestore collection Ltd (c); Photos 12 / © 2008 Disney / Pixar / © Disney (ca). **Corbis:** Steve Schapiro (cl). 106 **Corbis:** (t).
110–111 **Dreamstime.com:** Tacettin Ulas (b). 112 **Dreamstime.com:** Ben Heys (t). 116–117 **Dreamstime.com:** Qingwaa (b).
118 **Dreamstime.com:** Valeriya Smidt (tl). 120–121 **Dreamstime.com:** Buriy.
Jacket images: Front: Corbis: Ron Miller / Stocktrek Images, Walter Myers / Stocktrek Images br;
Dreamstime.com: Ambientideas ca; **Back: Alamy Images:** Eddie Toro cr; **Dreamstime.com:** Plutonius cla;
Fotolia: gubh83 t; **Spine: Corbis:** NASA / JPL-Caltech

All other images © Dorling Kindersley
For further information see: www.dkimages.com

Discover more at
www.dk.com

Contents

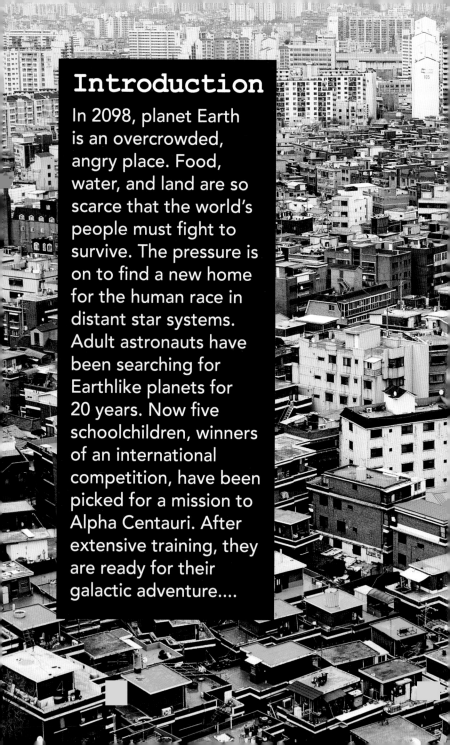

Introduction

In 2098, planet Earth is an overcrowded, angry place. Food, water, and land are so scarce that the world's people must fight to survive. The pressure is on to find a new home for the human race in distant star systems. Adult astronauts have been searching for Earthlike planets for 20 years. Now five schoolchildren, winners of an international competition, have been picked for a mission to Alpha Centauri. After extensive training, they are ready for their galactic adventure....

Star Facts
Alpha Centauri

The third brightest star in the night sky is, in fact, two stars, A and B, making up the closest star system to our solar system. It is seen in the Southern Hemisphere. Follow the crossbar of the Southern Cross to the left and it is the second bright star in the sky.

SOUTHERN CROSS

ALPHA CENTAURI

☆ The light from Alpha Centauri takes four years to reach Earth.
☆ ☆ It's the brightest in the constellation of Centaurus.
☆ ☆ ☆ The star system may contain at least one Earthlike planet.

100 Years of Global Warming, 1988–2088

Since the end of the 20th century, climate scientists have been concerned about the data and facts that indicated planet Earth is warming. The Intergovernmental Panel on Climate Change (IPCC) was formed in 1988 to provide the world's governments with a scientific view on the current state and future impact on the environment. In their centenary year, this report demonstrates the climate change over the past 100 years.

FACTS
- Average temperature of Earth has risen 10.4°F (5.8°C)
- Sea levels risen 1.9 feet (0.59 m)

CAUSES
- Burning of fossil fuels release carbon dioxide and other greenhouse gases into the atmosphere
- Agriculture and land clearing
- Human transportation and technology activities
- Natural variations, especially due to super-volcanic eruption in 2049

ENVIRONMENTAL IMPACT

- 35% of plant and animal species now extinct
- A further 60% of plant and animal species at risk
- Marine- and land-based plants and animals migrated toward the poles
- Polar ice caps melted
- Mountain glaciers in Asia and North America disappeared
- Increase in severe storms and weather events
- Increase in frequency of forest fires

SOCIOECONOMIC IMPACT

- Soaring summer temperatures in Northern and Southern Hemispheres cause heat stroke and deaths
- 80% of year are now "code red" air-quality days due to near-surface ozone and smoke across all continents
- Intense droughts cause malnutrition across continents
- Fresh water is scarce in 85% of the world
- Antarctica is now the most populated continent per landmass on Earth

Despite the IPCC's findings, predictions, and warnings over the past 100 years, the inevitable effects of global warming are now unstoppable.

Chapter 1

Into Orbit

It was still early morning when the blue minibus pulled up outside the hotel, but the Sun was already high in the sky. There was a steamy warmth like a sauna revving up.

"Let's go!" said Jason, and his class of five astronauts grabbed their luggage in an excited scramble. When the hotel doors opened, they jostled to be the first outside.

Jason pressed his thumb against the pad on the side of the minibus, and clambered on board. He waved to the rest of them to follow him. Then he leaned across and spoke into the vehicle's console.

"Vehicle, to the space tether, please."

The map on the display updated instantly, showing the most direct route to the destination.

"Confirmed. The journey will take approximately… twenty-five minutes, taking into account current traffic… strikes and riots."

"Y'all ready?" Jason drawled.

He didn't have to ask. None of his young students could wait a moment longer.

"OK vehicle. Close doors. Proceed."

The minibus edged away from the curb. It accelerated quickly onto the highway and cruised west.

It didn't take long to leave the high-rise buildings of the city behind. They sped past shabby houses with colorful washing and scorched dirt lawns.

Farther on, someone had sprayed some words on a wall. Underneath, the same words were written in English: we are hungry!

Then past a parade of burned-out cars, some still smoking. Black-clad cops in flak jackets waved the traffic on.

When they reached the countryside, the colors changed to shades of green. A thousand sprinklers threw rainbows above the fields. The road changed, too. The minibus slowed to weave around potholes.

Almost as soon as they had left the hotel, the crew had begun scanning the horizon for a view of the space tether. Casper spotted it first.

"There! Look. There it is."

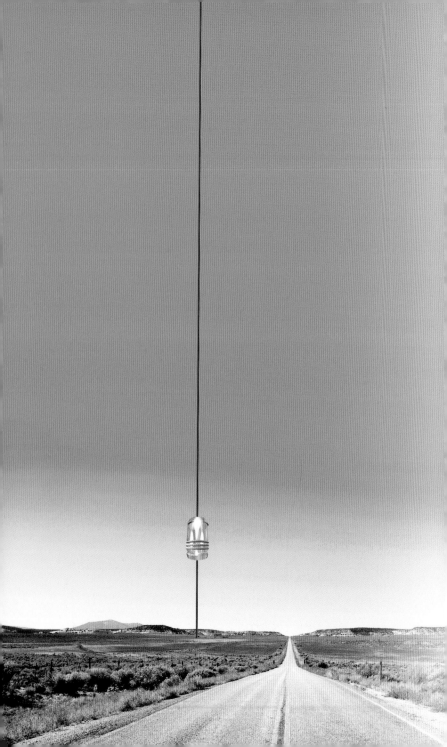

From where they were, the tether just looked like a dark red line. It rose straight and vertical on the horizon. It seemed to tie the sky down to the ground so that it would not blow away.

"Wow!" said Jude.

The minibus sped closer and closer. At the base, high metal gates whirred open. They were waved through security and drove to a complex of low buildings. They clambered out of the minibus and stared upward. From here, the gleaming red cable was almost too bright to look at.

Maria from France gazed in wonder. "It's like… how do you call it? The Indian rope trick? The magician, he throws the rope in the air and it stays up, tight. Then he climbs up it and disappears!"

"And that," said Hirohito, "is exactly what we are going to be doing in less than two hours."

For now though, the Sun's heat had burned away their curiosity. They hurried into the air-conditioned shade of the reception building.

Jason was standing just inside the door next to a tall woman wearing a green jumpsuit.

"This is Rachel," introduced Jason. "She is the android who is going to be the seventh member of our crew."

Hirohito giggled and nudged Casper. "Wow! She's nothing like the android we have to clean for us at home in Osaka. She's kind of, more…"

"Human?" said Lucy, completing his sentence.

"Yeah," said Jude. "You wouldn't know she was an android."

Lucy stepped forward and took Rachel's arm. "Hi Rachel! Great to have you on the team!" Then they all followed Jason into the complex.

It took them very little time to prepare for the launch. When they were all suited up, an engineer took them over to the elevator room.

"The tether has been up for eight years, now, so getting into orbit is routine. No costly, noisy rockets any more. We send up a lot of commercial crews, and bring them down again, of course!" he laughed. "Plus scientists, quite a few tourists, and the garbage team are regulars."

"The garbage team?" asked Hirohito.

"It's pretty messy up there," continued the engineer. "Of course there are strict regulations now about pollution, but for the first century of space exploration, you could dump whatever you liked. So, we have to clean it all up. You can't imagine what comes down—everything from nuclear reactors to specks of freeze-dried pee. They are from the Gemini program back in the 1960s."

"That's totally vintage!" said Hirohito.

"That's totally YUCK!" Lucy added.

"The cabin is pressurized, of course, so suits are just a precaution. We have a 100 percent safety record here."

The engineer opened the elevator cabin doors. "However..." he continued, pausing to make sure they were all listening, "... in orbit, everything is moving at two miles a second. Going that fast, something as small as a plum has the energy of a sixteen-wheel truck speeding down the fast lane. So keep your helmets sealed until you are safe inside Space Bace. Don't worry, though. Safe journey to orbit!"

Maria leaned across to Casper's ear. "Wow! Did you see that? He crossed his fingers."

They filed on board and took their seats—then all spent much longer than usual checking their suits and helmet seals. Finally, they were ready. The cabin doors hissed shut, and the red light above changed first to yellow, then green.

The cabin juddered slightly, rose slowly a yard or so, then stopped.

"Oh!" stammered Casper. "We're not going!"

Then, with a lurch, they soared upward. Up through the portal in the roof of the building; up into the deep blue, cloudless sky.

Lucy tried to clap, but the palms of her thick suit gloves just made a dull, quiet noise. "We have lift off!"

"Oh Lucy, that's sooo twentieth-century," said Jude.

The capsule gathered speed. Soon, the horizon was no longer a straight line. It began to dip at the edges into an elegant curve as they approached the edge of space.

It was a jaw-dropping, pulse-racing, unforgettable experience… at first. But the journey through the atmosphere and into orbit took the whole day.

20

By the time the cabin slowed on the approach to Space Bace, all six humans were asleep.

Rachel woke them. "We're here, team," she announced.

The elevator docked with the orbiting space station, and the seven passengers waited impatiently for the air pressure to equalize. They had left gravity behind on Earth, so when the doors opened, they just floated through into the entrance area of Space Bace.

Once inside, their excited chatter stopped for a moment.

Then Hirohito said, "It's absolutely like the simulator. I was expecting that it would be… somehow… cooler."

They all laughed because that was what they had all been thinking.

When they had taken off their suits and had something to eat, they went around the station looking out through

the viewports. On one side, the Earth was the blue marble familiar from photographs and training videos.
On the other side, they stared out at the gleaming craft, *Argo*, that would power them beyond the solar system tomorrow. Then, exhausted from the journey, they went to bed.

QUESTION
What words has the author used to describe the journey on the space tether? What other words would you have used?

Space Elevator

Traveling at 1,250 miles (2,000 km) per hour, the space tether elevator takes 18 hours to travel to the Space Bace in outer space. The elevator was a huge technological challenge, but its successful construction has revolutionized space travel. Powered by laser beams, shining onto power cells on its base, the streamlined elevator whizzes upward, carrying people and cargo through the atmosphere into outer space.

Anchor on Earth
At the base, the elevator cable is tethered to a sturdy platform designed to withstand the extreme stresses of the fast-moving elevator. The anchor in space provides tension to balance the weight of the cable.

ANCHOR
IN SPACE

SPACE
BACE

Space Bace
Orbiting at 22,000 miles (36,000 km) above Earth, the base is the first stop for space exploration.

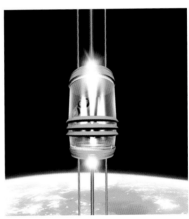

ELEVATOR

CABLE

ANCHOR
ON EARTH

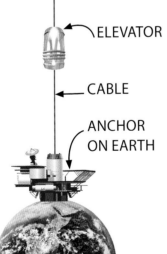

Elevator
This airtight capsule elevates at high speed along high-strength, lightweight cables.

Designed to Suit

Since the beginning of space travel, space suits have provided life support in the hostile conditions of space. However, designs continue to improve, enhanced by new materials with useful properties and additional accessories.

To protect from dangers, a space suit must:
- be airtight and pressurized,
- provide oxygen and remove carbon dioxide,
- maintain a comfortable temperature with cooling system and ventilation,
- deflect a star's heat and be flame-resistant,
- must not tear and must prevent damage from micrometeoroids,
- allow good vision and protection from the glare of the stars,
- enable easy movement inside and outside of the spacecraft,
- allow communication with others.

Apollo A7L
1969–1972

Sokol KV-2 ("Falcon")
1980–present

Extravehicular mobility unit (EMU)
1982–present

Chapter 2

All Aboard?

The first morning aboard Space Bace began with the low red glow of the dormitory night lights turning slowly yellow, then bright white.

Tethered in red sleeping bags, the crew looked like the pupae of some huge moth. Casper was the first to really wake up.

"How did you sleep, Hirohito?"

"Huh? What…? Oh, right, yeah.

Dreadful. Even with earplugs in, I couldn't get used to the humming fans and bleeping alerts. The silence of space? The guy who wrote that hasn't been up here!"

Hirohito, wriggling, pulled himself to the viewport. "Wow! What a view!"

22,000 miles below them, a brilliant crescent of land and sea glistened and glimmered above the black shadow where the Sun had yet to rise.

Hirohito's delighted cry brought the rest of the crew struggling from sleep to take a look, and they all jostled for the best view.

An hour later, they had washed, dressed, and eaten their first space breakfast.

"OK," said Jason, "we have all looked at our schedules, so we know what we are doing this morning. It's your final day of training. You've been through all the procedures a hundred times before in the simulator and in the float pool, but this time it's for real."

He turned and headed for *Argo*. The glass door of the airlock swung open, and he pulled himself through the short tunnel into the craft.

The rest of the crew followed. They fell easily into the routines they had studied so carefully. Lucy crouched over the propulsion console. Jude handled

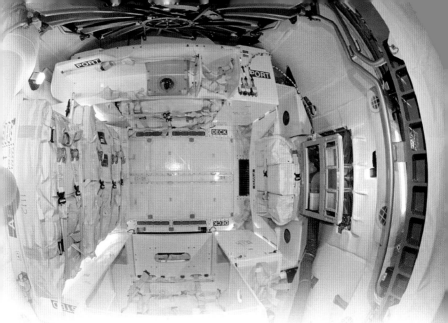

communications on the comm's link.
Casper powered up the navigation
computer. Maria was in charge of life
support. Hirohito and Jason sat at
the command and control stations.

   For an hour, each of them ran
checks and diagnostics, and checked
off their lists.

QUESTION
What role would you like to have
on a spacecraft?

"Are we all through?" asked Jason. He looked around the circle of faces nodding back at him. "Great! Good to go, then."

There was a whoop of excitement. Hirohito high-fived Lucy, and the others hugged in a tangled ball of limbs. Still unused to the microgravity, it took a moment for them to pull themselves apart, laughing together.

"Wait a minute," said Jason. "This has to be a photo-op. I'll go and get my camera." He drifted off back through the tunnel.

"I just can't quite believe we're actually going to do it…" began Lucy.

"Yay, too right!" said Casper. "How about… going right now?"

With a jokey drama, he flipped up a safety cover on the command console, and rested his finger on the large red button beneath it.

Lucy's jaw dropped. "Casper! Don't! Not even as a joke!" She lunged toward him to pull his hand away.

In a dreadful, fumbling crunch that they would all remember later in slow-motion, she jostled Hirohito and Jude. In turn, they slammed up against Casper, whose extended fingertip made hard and positive contact with the red launch button.

Across the cabin from the spinning figures, they heard the gentle whirr of the two airlock doors closing. Then a less familiar—and much louder—metallic clunk. A dozen titanium bolts slammed home, solidly locking and sealing the doors. There was the briefest of flashes as small explosive charges cut the four rods holding *Argo* to the orbital base.

"Shoot! We're, like, separated!" Jude called out.

At that very moment, Jason's face appeared at one of the windows on Space Bace. His eyes were wide in an expression of complete panic. Almost immediately, he disappeared again and the comm's link beeped into life.

"OK guys, I'm not blaming anybody. I don't want to know how this happened. Let's just find a way to get you back here and docked with the base again."

Lucy swiped at the glass surface of the mission manual pad strapped to her leg. "Hey, yeah, well, docking and return was on day... day 532 of our schedule. Let's all take a look at that screen and start the routines."

They hustled to their stations as Jason broke in again. "And I guess as soon as you're back through the tunnel, we'd better get you back down the tether and figure out what went wrong."

The frantic activity in *Argo* suddenly stopped.

"He said… what?!" they gasped.

Jason heard them over the comm's link.

"Well, of course, we can't go on with the mission. The separation bolts will have to be replaced, and…"

Lucy leaned over and pressed mute.

"Guys, we need to have a really serious talk about this."

It didn't take long for the five of them to make up their minds:

"I'm not going back."

"We've trained for 18 months for this moment."

"Sorry, guys. I was just messing around."

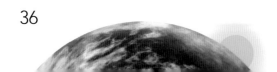

"Just wait…" said Hirohito, "can Jason still control *Argo* from Space Bace?"

"Not any more!" Lucy grinned broadly, pointing at the main control screen, where "MANUAL COMMAND" was flashing red.

"OK then," sighed Hirohito. "We all know what to do."

They hustled to their stations, sat down, and tightened their straps.

"I'm not going to count this down," said Hirohito. "Is everybody ready?"

Without waiting for a reply, he lifted the cover on the relativity drive control and grasped the T-shaped joystick that would blast them across the universe.

QUESTION
Why did the students decide to go on?

Argo Spacecraft

Thruster

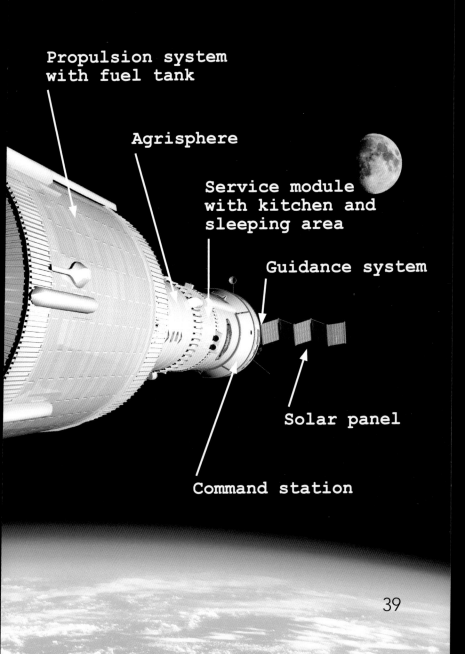

Propulsion system
with fuel tank

Agrisphere

Service module
with kitchen and
sleeping area

Guidance system

Solar panel

Command station

39

Hirohito's Space Blog

Goodbye, Earth!

Woke up this morning, and the first thing I did was to look out of the viewport. Couldn't help but wonder at the sight of the Earth below. I could see the curved horizon against the black background of space. The edge of Earth was smeared out though due to the atmosphere. The width of the atmosphere was about the width of my index finger held out at arm's length. The Pacific Ocean was a deep bright blue color and there were scattered bright white clouds over the equator.

The sunrise was beautiful with very thin, distinct color layers in the atmosphere. These ranged from orange and red near the surface to various shades of blue, purple, and finally black. The Sun rose very quickly. When the Sun was low in the sky, the high clouds cast long shadows over the ground.

On the night sides of the Earth, I could see the yellow glow of the cities' lights and lights along major roads. There was a spectacular thunderstorm over the southern Indian Ocean. The lightning flashes illuminated the clouds from within. The aurora over Antarctica looked like a glowing green curtain, wafting upward at the top of the atmosphere.

Must sign off as about to do final preparations on board *Argo* ahead of our launch to new frontiers.

Sayõnara (*Goodbye*)

INTERSTELLAR TRAVEL

THE CHALLENGE

To travel between stars in months rather than in years.

THE FACTS

1 light-year = 5,868 billion miles (9,460 billion km)

Speed of light = 186,000 miles/s (approx 300,000 km/s)

Size of our solar system = more than 1 light-year

Alpha Centauri = 4.35 light-years away

Size of Milky Way galaxy = 100,000 light-years

Andromeda Galaxy (nearest galaxy)
= 2.5 million light-years away

DEFINITIONS
- A **light-year** is the distance that light travels in a year. This is used as a unit of measuring distances in space.
- **Warp** is a bending or curving of space. At the start of the 21st century, this is still unproven.
- A **g-force** is a measurement of acceleration equal to the force of gravity on an object (i.e. its weight).

A FEW OF THE OPTIONS

FASTER-THAN-LIGHT TRAVEL

A spacecraft uses the curving of space to take a "shortcut" from one point to another. The curve would be like a wave in which a spaceship would be carried in a warp bubble, as if on a magic carpet. The wave is due to the gravitational effect of spacetime being compressed in front of the craft and expanding behind it.

LASER PROPULSION

A spacecraft is propelled by lasers that warp spacetime to attract and repel itself like a magnet. This would mean that distances between points could be eliminated and so making it possible to be in two places at the same time.

CONSTANT ACCELERATION

An engine-powered spacecraft stays accelerating at more than 1 g-force. The craft pushes forward for the first half of the journey, reaching the speed of light. Then it uses backthrust for the last half, so that it arrives at the destination at a standstill. A typical person loses consciousness at about 5 g-force.

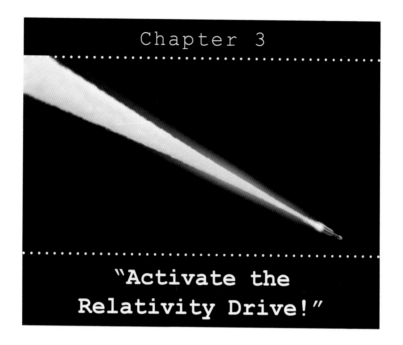

Chapter 3

"Activate the Relativity Drive!"

Hirohito pressed in the safety lock at the top of the lever and eased it forward. As power surged to the relativity drive, the sudden acceleration pushed everyone back into their seats.

It was a moment they had prepared for, but they had never experienced g-forces this high—not even in the huge centrifuge that flung them in tight circles back at the training base.

44

"Yeouch!" whispered Casper, fighting to catch his breath. "I had no idea it would be this uncomfortable."

"Don't worry, Cas," Lucy reassured him. "It will ease off once we reach cruising velocity."

Casper had to struggle just to nod his head in reply.

The discomfort was not the only effect of the massively powerful drive. As the craft reached and exceeded light speeds, the crew lost contact with Earth. They left behind the slower radio signals that kept them in touch with ground stations and the orbiting Space Bace.

When their speed had risen high enough, Hirohito eased the joystick back. *Argo*'s acceleration slowed and stopped. From feeling several times their Earth-bound weight, the astronauts again floated weightlessly.

They unclipped their belts.

"Cabin crew doors to automatic and cross-check," joked Lucy, miming an airline stewardess.

Their laughter made them all relax, and they gazed at the mission manuals on their leg pads. They swiped through the screens for a while, and then Casper spoke, "Without Jason, we are one crew member down. There will be more work for the rest of us, but I think we can probably manage."

He scratched his head and turned another page. "I suggest that Hirohito is in command for our first week," he continued. "Then I'll take over, then Jude, and so on, changing every week."

"Hey, have we really thought this out?" Jude butted in. "Don't you think we should discuss... turning back? It will be much harder once we leave the solar system."

There was an awkward moment, and then Lucy said quietly, "Hirohito, why don't you and I go and check the agrisphere. The g-forces may have shaken some of our little passengers out of their homes."

The pair of them headed for the tunnel to the food production pod.

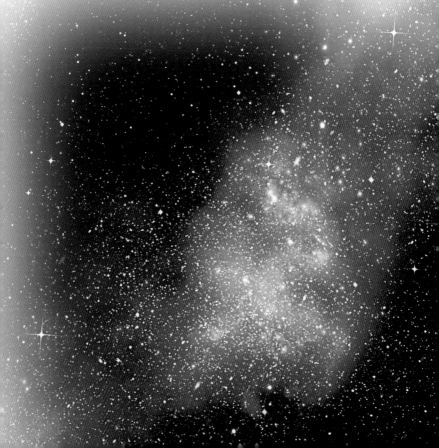

After the cramped interior of
the control cabin, the agrisphere
seemed like a green, leafy paradise.
They basked for a minute in the Sun's
weak rays before starting their tasks.

The two of them worked in silence
for a while. They picked dead leaves
from the crop plants and checked
the irrigation system for dry spots.

Then Lucy said, "What do you think about Jude, Hirohito? He's obviously not comfortable. I didn't get that buzz off him in training."

"Maybe he's right to worry. After all, we have just stolen a trillion-dollar intergalactic craft! Hey, look at the time. We had better grab supper."

They picked the biggest of the salad leaves, and then moved to a netted area.

"Mmm! These little critters look ready for the pot!" said Lucy. She reached inside the net and began picking off the silkworm grubs.

"It's a shame we can't deep-fry them with chili and garlic," said Hirohito. "I love them served like that."

"Yeah, but all that hot oil in microgravity?" said Lucy. "Shame. My grandma told me that pork tastes a lot like silkworm grubs. Have you ever eaten pork?"

"No," Hirohito replied thoughtfully, "but my mom can remember eating beef when there was still enough land to keep mammals in fields."

They closed the netting, checked the nutrient and water-supply levels, and carefully edged their way back to the command capsule.

Inside the kitchen area, Rachel was already busy preparing the meal. She washed the grubs and lettuce leaves separately. "Hey, we don't want our main course to eat our salad!"

To someone who had never seen a busy android at work, Rachel's speed would have seemed unreal. As she chopped, the knife was a metallic blur. No human chef could have worked as fast without cutting off a fingertip.

Steamed and microwaved, the meal was soon ready. Rachel presented it with a flourish. "Spicy silkworm ragout with quinoa and green salad."

They all began eating hungrily.

"Thanks, Rachel, this is delicious!" said Maria. "It sure beats the pizza from my local pizzeria in Paris."

QUESTION
What impression has the author given you about each crew member? Which one would you get along with and who would you not trust?

Cosmic Gardening

Plants can be grown for fresh food in space, and, just like on Earth, plants create a lush, calm environment for people to enjoy and to stimulate senses.

Challenges
Plants need water, carbon dioxide, and nutrients, and some gravity to prevent growth problems. Also plants may need a little help to pollinate.

Types of plants grown
Plants are chosen for providing a plentiful crop in small spaces e.g. thale cress, lentils, wheat, leafy green plants, field mustard plants, soybeans, strawberries, peppers, cucumbers, and herbs.

Streamlined layout for limited space.

Insects eat the parts inedible for humans, producing fertilizer and providing a cycle of nutrients.

Some insects such as silkworms provide astronauts with other useful benefits.

Low power and long-lasting LED lights produce artificial lighting. As these lights don't get hot, they can be placed close to the plants, shedding light under and around the leaves. The lighting can also be customized for different plant types.

Robots help pollinate.

Air and humidity supply is regulated.

Rotating plant beds provide artificial gravity.

Plants can be used to purify water and recycle carbon dioxide into oxygen.

Plants are grown in soil-free hydroponic cultures that provide a recirculating stream of nutrients in the water.

Products from Space

At this very moment, you could be using something that was first used in space.

Scratch-resistant lenses
A coating of special plastic was created while improving helmet visors for astronauts. This is now used for eyeglasses and sunglasses.

Swipe card strips
This technology was developed when creating multiple onboard systems on spacecraft for recognizing data being received.

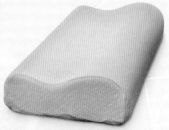

Memory foam
This foam can be compressed fully and then changes back to its original form. Created for spacecraft seats to lessen the impact during landings, it is now used in mattresses, padding for motorcycle seats, and protection for race car drivers.

Space boot foam
Now used in athletic shoes, this foam fabric spreads out the force on a person's feet when walking or running.

Satellite technology

The first satellites were designed to find out about outer space and to communicate this information with people on Earth. Now, around 200 communication satellites orbit the globe each day.

Infared sensor thermometers

The technology used for measuring the temperature of stars is now used for taking quick temperature readings from patients' ear drums in hospitals.

Cordless power

Inspired by the power supply designed for NASA's Apollo mission, cordless tools use a battery-powered, magnet-motor drill with a computer program, reducing the amount of power and maximizing battery life.

Water filters

Developed for long space flights to clean water, the filters are used to purify tap water in homes.

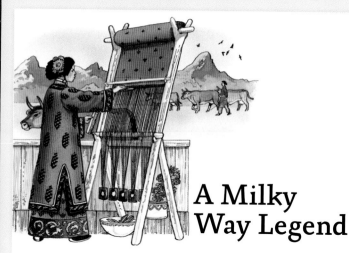

A Milky Way Legend

Our solar system and the stars of Alpha Centauri are on the edge of the Milky Way galaxy. From Earth, the Milky Way with its bright band of light from all its stars is seen as a glowing arch. Two stars Altair and Vega shine brightly on either side. These separated stars have inspired a Chinese legend.

The Jade Emperor, ruler of Heaven, had a beautiful daughter Chih Nu. Her gift was to weave the most exquisite cloth for her father's robes, using clouds, the Sun's rays, and twinkling stars.

One summer's day, she caught sight of the handsome herdsman, Niu Lang, leading the royal cattle along the banks of the river. The Jade Emperor allowed them to marry.

Chih Nu and Niu Lang were so devoted to each other that they neglected their duties. The weaving wheel gathered cobwebs and the royal cattle wandered, destroying the heaven's meadows and crops. This angered the Jade Emperor. Despite their pleadings, he separated them, banishing Niu Lang to the other side of the river.

After a while, the Jade Emperor took a little pity on them and allowed Chih Nu and Niu Lang to meet once a year on the seventh day of the seventh month. On that day, crows gathered from around the world and formed a bridge for them over the river.

Milky Way

On Chinese Valentine's Day, the Milky Way appears dimmer, so that the two stars are not separated from each other.

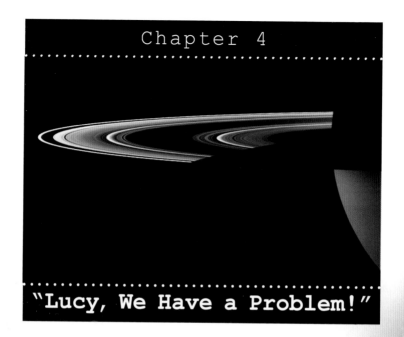

Chapter 4

"Lucy, We Have a Problem!"

There was plenty to keep the crew busy, and at the end of the day they flopped gratefully into their sleeping stations. *Argo* was quieter than Space Bace and they all slept better.

In the morning, Hirohito had set a personal alarm, and he slowly turned up the lights to wake his team-mates. Over breakfast he outlined the challenges for the day ahead.

"OK, guys, we're only 24 hours into our mission, but we already have a big hurdle to cross. We're about an hour away from Saturn. We are going to use the planet's gravity to make a course correction. So as navigator, you're going to be busy, Casper."

"OK, I think I can handle it," replied Casper.

"Thanks," continued Hirohito. "You'll all remember from training that Saturn's going to do something else for us. The planet's mass is going to give us an extra burst of speed. We're going to use it like a slingshot, swinging around it and then zooming off again. Let's make sure we come through this without a scratch."

Moments later, the cabin was briefly abuzz with activity, as everybody got to work. Then silence, as concentration replaced chat. Even Rachel had been given a task, taking the second seat at the command console where Jason would have been sitting.

Lucy let out a yell. "Ouch! Looks like we have a coolant leak. It's around the back of the agrisphere."

"How fast?" Casper sounded worried.

"Not so fast… can't say exactly, but I'd guess about… a quart an hour."

"I'm on it," Hirohito called across. "I'm launching a bot. Check out channel three for visual."

Everyone switched their monitors to the robot's video feed. They watched as it puttered and hissed its way down the tangle of gantries and girders.

It took Hirohito a couple of minutes to steer the bot to the right location.

"Bot on the spot, Lucy. Anybody see anything unusual?"

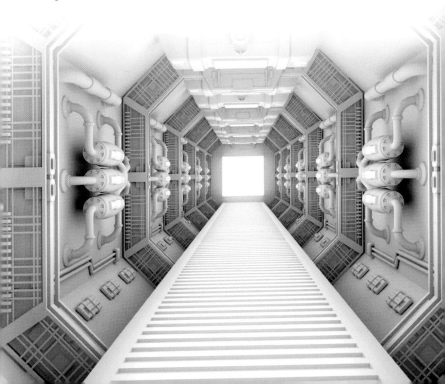

"I'm glad there's nothing unusual," Lucy said. "Nope. Nothing to see."

"Nothing's more worrying than something." Hirohito's knuckles were white where he gripped the bot controller, and he was rushing his words out. His anxiety was infectious.

Casper furrowed his brows, leaned closer to his console, and typed rapidly. "Hold on… I'm running… I'll just try a couple of diagnostic routines... Relax, guys. There's no leak. It's a busted pressure sensor. Look, Hiro, we can just swap this out…?"

He turned, expecting that everyone would be looking at their screens, but they weren't. They were all staring the other way, toward the main command console. Jude was standing in front of it, blocking the cabin.

"I'm really sorry to let you down, guys, but this is as far as we go," Jude began.

"Without Jason here, and without a comm's link to Earth, this mission is just too dangerous. I've set a different course correction. In five minutes, we're going to swing around the back of Saturn. We'll be back home in a day…"

Then he added, "…an Earth day, that is. Saturn days are ten times longer," and laughed nervously. "And there's one more thing. Rachel's with me, too. I'm sure I don't need to remind you that, as a model C7/95P, she has the strength of two adult human males."

"That's right." Rachel's perfectly synthesized voice was calm and determined. "Don't interfere. I don't want to have to hurt any of you."

Casper spoke up. "This is a very foolish step to take."

Jude scowled at him.

"I'm not willing to negotiate on this. I'm…"

"Quiet, Jude, I'm not talking to you," Casper interrupted. "Rachel, I want you to listen very carefully," he said slowly and firmly.

The android turned obediently to face Casper. The brave expression she had worn a moment before was suddenly gone. She brushed a wisp of her hair from her forehead.

"Yes, Casper, I am listening."

Lucy leaned toward her console.

Jude spun around. "Nobody touch ANYTHING!"

"It's OK, Jude, I'm just setting a timer," said Lucy, in a steady voice. She swiped the glass face of her pad. "Casper, we have two minutes, forty seconds left."

He nodded.

"Rachel, you know what the three laws are, don't you?"

"Yes, Casper, of course I do."

"Then please repeat the first law to me."

"An android will never injure a human being."

Casper paused for a moment and Jude butted in, "Casper, don't waste your time. Rachel won't listen to you."

Casper ignored him. "Rachel, listen very carefully," he said again.

"One minute seventeen," Lucy called across the cabin.

Casper raised his hand and kept staring at Rachel. "Now please do this for me. Go to the console and abort the course correction set by Jude."

"Don't do it, Rachel!" Jude shot the android an angry glance.

"I am sorry, Jude. I must obey Casper."

"Twenty-two seconds."

Rachel turned to the console and in a couple of deft moves canceled the command.

Jude crumpled onto a bench, and then slunk off to the dormitory.

"We won't forget this!" Hirohito called after him.

"Phew!" Lucy gasped. "Casper, how did you pull that one off?"

Casper just shrugged. "It wasn't really that tough. I'm a bit geeky, and I did a term paper on androids. I managed to download a manual for a model similar to Rachel's. I remembered the control

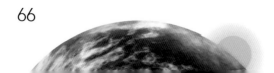

sequence to use for instructions that an android must obey. You use their name, and then before the command you say 'listen very carefully'. It was just a lucky break, really."

QUESTION
What words has the author used to convey Jude's manner through the conflict? Were they effective?

Saturn Slingshot

To save fuel and yet achieve high speeds and change direction, spacecraft can use the gravitational pull of a planet, such as Saturn, to propel it onward to the outer planets of the solar system, and beyond.

**4 mi/s
(7 km/s)**

**5 mi/s
(8 km/s)**

**STAGE 2:
THE
SLINGSHOT**
The spacecraft uses the gravitational pull of the planet to whisk around, picking up more speed, for example, to 6 miles per second (9 km/s).

**6 mi/s
(9 km/s)**

**5 mi/s
(8 km/s)**

STAGE 1: THE APPROACH
The spacecraft approaches the planet at increasing speed. For example, from 3–5 miles per second (6–8 km/s) . The planet is moving in the opposite direction.

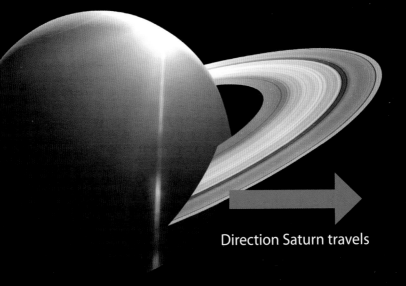

**4 mi/s
(7 km/s)**

**3 mi/s
(6 km/s)**

**3 mi/s
(6 km/s)**

Direction Saturn travels

STAGE 3: THE DEPARTURE
The spacecraft leaves the orbit of the planet at a constant faster speed of 5 miles per second (8 km/s), without needing to use up fuel.

**5 mi/s
(8 km/s)**

**5 mi/s
(8 km/s)**

Timeline of Space Exploration

October 4, 1957
Launch of *Sputnik 1*, the world's first artificial satellite.

November 3, 1957
Soviet dog Laika becomes first living creature in space.

February 3, 1966
Soviet's *Luna 9* becomes first craft to land successfully on the Moon.

July 20, 1969
US astronaut Neil Armstrong becomes first person to walk on the Moon.

July 20, 1976
US spacecraft *Viking 1* becomes first craft to land successfully on Mars.

1950   **1960**   **1970**   **1980**

October 10, 1959
Soviet spacecraft *Luna 3* returns first pictures of the Moon's far side.

April 12, 1961
Soviet cosmonaut Yuri Gagarin becomes the first person in space.

February 20, 1962
John Glenn becomes first US astronaut to orbit the Earth.

March 18, 1965
First space walk by Soviet cosmonaut Alexei Leonov.

October 18, 1967
Soviet's *Venera 4* becomes first craft to land on Venus.

September 1, 1979
US spacecraft *Pioneer 11* makes first flyby of Saturn.

March 29, 1974
US spacecraft *Mariner 10* makes first flyby of Mercury.

December 3, 1973
US spacecraft *Pioneer 10* makes first flyby of Jupiter.

April 19, 1971
Launch of Soviet's *Salyut 1*—the world's first space station.

January 24, 1986
US spacecraft *Voyager 2* makes first flyby of Uranus.

August 25, 1989
Voyager 2 makes first flyby of Neptune.

Voyager 2

1990   2000   2010   2020

November 20, 1998
Launch of the first part of the *International Space Station.*

April 24, 1990
Launch of the Hubble Space Telescope from Space Shuttle *Discovery.*

2015
A robotic spacecraft is set to be the first to fly by and study Pluto and its Moons.

Hubble Space Telescope

Pluto from the Hubble Space Telescope

71

ROBOTIC ARMS

These robots can mimic human movements. They can also carry out tasks that are too dangerous for humans.

SPIDERLIKE ROBOT

These are created to explore terrain inaccessible to rovers with wheels.

ROVERS
These are used to transmit information back to Earth as they explore and analyze the surface of planets.

ASTRONAUT RESCUE ROBOT
If a space-walking astronaut breaks a tether while outside a ship, this robot comes to the rescue.

Chapter 5

An Amazing Discovery

Within a couple of days of their hasty, unofficial, and illegal departure from Earth, *Argo* was on the extreme edges of the solar system. The Sun's rays were too weak to warm the craft and the crew. Even the glittering glass agrisphere needed bright lights to keep crops and grubs growing.

Two days later, the Sun had shrunk to a distant speck.

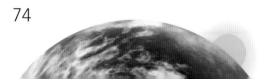

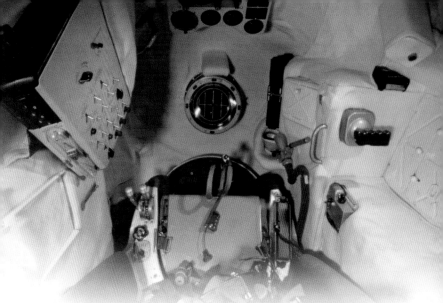

Days on board *Argo* turned to weeks. Weeks turned to months. The cabin, which had been so neat when they boarded, became messy and slightly dirty. Discarded clothes and tiny balls of fluff floated in out-of-the-way corners.

The life-support system recirculated clean air every five minutes, but still there was a stale smell.

The mood was stale, too. The crew talked less. After a few arguments, everyone had learned which subjects to avoid speaking about.

So on day 298, at 11:53 in the morning, nobody paid much attention when Lucy called Hirohito over to the command console. "Hiro, can I just run some figures past you?"

The shy kid from Osaka pulled himself across and floated next to Lucy. They pored over the screens together for half an hour.

"OK, guys, fuel update," announced Lucy, clapping her hands. "Looks like we are VERY close to not having enough power to complete the trip."

Maria wrinkled her brows. "But Lucy, we are almost there, and we have been coasting on zero power for the last three months."

Lucy nodded. "Yes, but we are traveling at three times the speed of light. We need power to slow down and we can't use a drogue parachute in space."

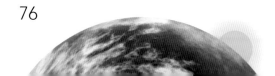

"Hey, hold on Lucy, just come and take a look at this for a moment," Casper interrupted.

One by one, they gathered at the viewport until its shiny surface reflected 12 attentive eyes.

"Just look at this blob here—" continued Casper, "the one in the exact center."

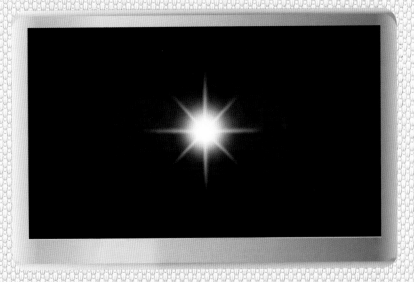

"If it's in the middle, it must be Alpha Centauri," said Jude.

"Yes, Jude, obviously it's the star we're heading for," replied Casper impatiently, "but what do you notice about it?"

"Ah!" said Jude. "It's become, like, an elongated blob, not just a dot any more."

"That's right!" Casper said. "We're close enough now to see, even without any magnification, that it's a binary star. Now watch this…"

He poked a button to turn on the optical telescope. A vivid image snapped onto the screen. Everyone gasped. It was Alpha Centauri as no human had ever seen it before. The two stars stood crisply apart.

"Now, look just here." Casper's fingertip drew a red circle on the screen. In the middle was a clump of blue pixels. "Want a closer look?"

They all nodded. Casper cranked up the magnification.

"It's a planet!" gasped Lucy.

"Yeah. All the evidence suggested it was there, but nobody was really sure—until now. Welcome to Earth 2.0!"

Then everything went a little crazy. They hugged; they whooped; they yelled. They spun themselves in tight somersaults in that way you can do only in microgravity.

After the momentary celebration, they all went back to the screen.

"Maria, you're the expert on life sciences. Can you run some tests for us?" asked Casper.

Maria elbowed her way to her workstation and began punching keys. "I think we're close enough to get some data. First thing to do is to put a scale on it." She dragged a ruler onto the screen.

"Looks promising," she continued. "Planetary radius of about 4,000 miles. Gravity is going to be pretty much the same as Earth. Maybe a little lower. We're all going to lose weight!"

She turned on the spectrograph, and in a couple of seconds, she was gazing at the planet's color signature. "There's strong absorption in the red A and B lines, so there's plenty of oxygen. More good news. We'll be able to breathe."

Maria punched a couple more buttons to change the range. She became more excited. "There's plenty of water, too!"

Casper pushed forward. "Can you get the surface temperature, Maria?"

"Hold on, I'll switch to infrared," she said, pressing the switches. "Uh-huh… here we go. Yes! Around 300 Kelvin!" She clapped her hands with delight, "It's a beautiful day on Earth 2.0!"

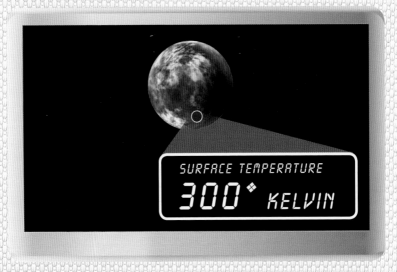

On the other side of the cabin, Hirohito raised his voice. "Let's not get too excited. I don't want to rain on your parade, but you seem to have forgotten the fuel problem that Lucy identified."

Everybody turned to face him and Lucy. It was Casper that asked the question that was in all their minds.

"Lucy, what does this marginal fuel thing mean?"

"Well, in the worst possible situation, it means that our braking maneuver might be terminated prematurely."

"Come on, Lucy. In PLAIN ENGLISH," Casper pleaded.

"It means that we might only get a brief glimpse of Earth 2.0 because we will be flying straight past at light speed. Then we will vanish forever into the dark, cold cosmos beyond."

The Birth and Death of Stars

1. Stars are born in swirling clouds of gas and dust called **nebulas**. Bright nebulas glow. Dark nebulas are foggy, shadowy shapes lit up by stars behind them.

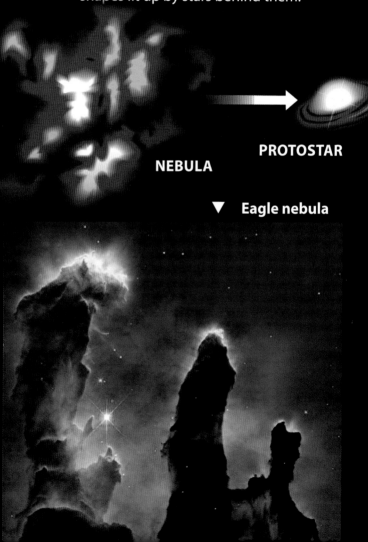

NEBULA

PROTOSTAR

▼ **Eagle nebula**

2. A star forms when gases in a nebula clump together into a tight, spinning ball. This **protostar** begins to glow as it gets hotter.

3. On average, stars use up all their fuel (heat) after about 10 billion years. Smaller stars shine for longer than larger ones.

4. After billions of years a middle-sized star, like the Sun, begins to cool down. It then swells up more than 100 times to become a **red giant**.

STAR

RED GIANT

WHITE DWARF

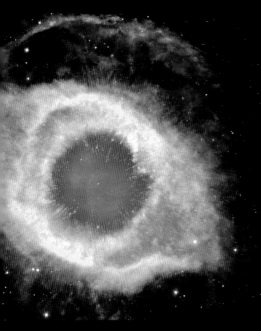

5. At the end of its life, a Sun-like star collapses into a **white dwarf**. A strange-shaped nebula of swirling gas and space dust remains around it, in which new stars may form one day.

◄ **Helix nebula around a white dwarf**

Dramatic Deaths of Stars

A large star glows very brightly. Toward the end of its life, it expands into a **supergiant**. Finally, it explodes in a blinding flash called a **supernova**.

▲ **Antares, red supergiant**

Most supernovas leave behind a tiny but very heavy **neutron star**. This is equivalent to a teaspoonful of salt weighing more than all the people on Earth.

▼ **Crab nebula with neutron star**

The biggest supernovas leave behind a mysterious object called a **black hole**. This is an invisible place in space where gravity is so strong that it works like a vacuum cleaner. Anything that comes near is pulled toward it. Nothing can escape a black hole— not even light.

Constellations

A constellation is a group of stars that appears to form a pattern or picture. These are easily recognizable patterns that help people find their way using the night sky. There are 88 named constellations.

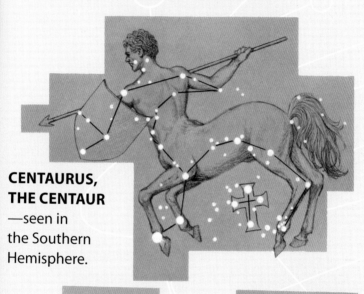

CENTAURUS, THE CENTAUR —seen in the Southern Hemisphere.

THE GREAT BEAR —seen most of the year in the Northern Hemisphere.

ORION

—seen throughout the world. This is one of the easiest constellations to spot with its pattern of three bright stars forming Orion's belt. Orion was a huge strong hunter, according to ancient Greek legend.

ANDROMEDA AND PERSEUS

—seen in the Northern Hemisphere. In myth, Perseus was an ancient Greek hero who rescued Andromeda from a sea serpent.

Chapter 6

Destination Earth 2.0

There was silence for a moment as they all tried to take in what Lucy had told them. They had just one chance to get their tiny craft into planetary orbit.

"Lucy, how did we get into this bind?"

"Well, Casper," Lucy replied, "it's not entirely clear. I have pored over the logs of our power use. I can't find any one thing that has devoured our supplies. It could be the agrisphere, though.

90

When we were still in the solar system, the Sun provided free energy, but in the darkness of deep space, heating and lighting the area takes a lot of power."

"We should not waste any more time analyzing this," Hirohito butted in. "We really have to crunch the numbers for the approach trajectory. We need to make doubly sure that we are captured by the planet's gravity."

His serious tone impressed the rest of the team as much as his words. They all hurried away to their consoles. Within half an hour, they were ready.

They had agreed that Casper had the best grasp of their status and progress, so he buckled himself into the command seat.

"Rachel, why don't you join me? I could do with your faultless logic and quick wits!" requested Casper.

The android grinned. "Thanks, Cas!" She took the seat next to him.

Their high speed had brought them quickly into the star system. Hirohito felt its warmth through the viewport by his seat. He remembered the Sun they had left behind and felt his first twinge of homesickness. He soon forgot it, though, as he ran through checklists for their approach.

"Hiro—you monitor our fuel status and let me know how we're doing," Casper called across.

"OK, Cas. Right now, we have about 102% of what we need to reach orbit.

FUEL TO REACH DESTINATION

102%

F   ½   E

That's a 2% safety margin. It's slim, but it should get us there."

"Fingers crossed, then."

Casper winked at Hiro, and lifted the safety cover on the relativity drive.

"Is everybody ready?"

He looked around the cabin, and they all nodded back at him.

"Good. Maria, how far off are we?"

"Approximately 85 seconds, Cas. Switch the drive to automatic. The flight computer will start the braking maneuver."

Casper pushed the lever to the side and they all waited. Nobody spoke.

The drive kicked in with a sickening jerk, throwing them forward against their harnesses. Lucy gasped at the pressure. Hirohito slumped forward in his seat.

"Hiro, are you OK?" Jude shook him anxiously.

"Uh?" Hiro opened his eyes slowly. "Yeah… Yes, don't worry. The g's got me there for a moment. I'll be fine."

He lifted his gaze up to the screen in front of him.

"Power's OK. We still have a 2% margin."

"Great!" Cas called back. "We've slowed to zero-point three g.
We should get a visual fix any time…"
He pointed to the viewport.
Sure enough, they could see the planet now as a distant blue speck.
It was growing rapidly, even though they were braking hard.

Then, suddenly, it disappeared.

"What! Where's it gone!?" Casper's eyes darted from his console to the viewport. "This can't be happening! We were just…"

He turned to Maria, who was frantically tapping her screen.

94

"Quoi! Ce n'est pas possible!"
Then, she repeated in English,
"The planet is still there. It's just
that… there is something in the way.
Probably an asteroid. Can we
make a course correction?"

"Too late for discussion!" said Lucy,
and swiftly pounding her screen, she
fired a lateral thruster on full power.

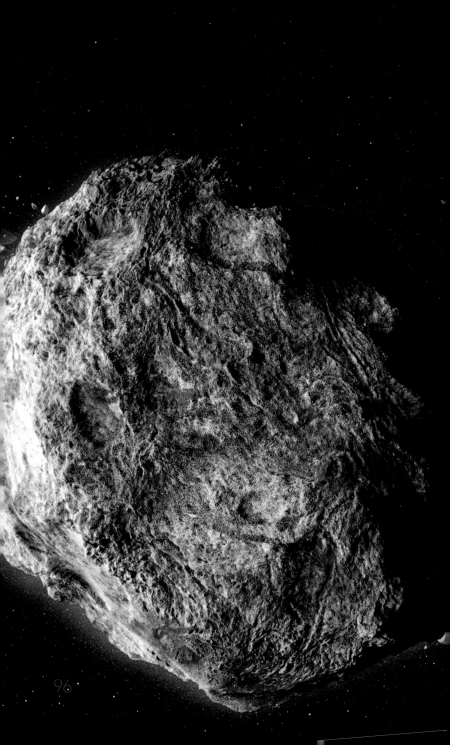

Argo lurched sideways. The asteroid was racing toward them fast. A couple of seconds earlier, it was a distant blip. Now it was a rocky giant, blocking their view of everything ahead.

"No!" Instinctively, Hirohito grabbed the console in front of him, bracing himself for the impact.

It never came. The asteroid soared past, and as swiftly as it had grown, it shrank again to a speck behind them.

Lucy shivered, "Phew! That was a close call!"

The rest of the crew slumped back in their seats, dizzy with relief.

But then Maria called across, "Cas, I don't think we're going to make it. We were close enough to that asteroid for its gravity to change our course. We may skip off the planet's atmosphere like a skipped stone off a lake. Can we stand on the brakes a bit more?"

FUEL TO REACH DESTINATION
100.5%

F · · · · · ½ · · · · E

Rachel spoke up now. "I don't advise that. The g's would not be a problem for androids, but the human body would suffer extreme stress."

Hirohito had a warning, too. "There's a fuel issue, Cas. Our safety margin has dropped to only 0.5%."

Cas wrinkled his brows for only a moment. "Sorry, guys, it's a tough call. If we miss this, there are no second chances."

Before anyone could disagree, he tapped the panel in front of him and slid the drive joystick from auto to manual.

The effect was immediate. It felt like hitting a wall. Everyone was flung forward so hard that their safety harnesses creaked and strained.

The straps dug hard into their flesh, but nobody cried out, for every human on *Argo* was unconscious. The g-forces had drained their brains of blood. Each one of them sank into an inky blackout where time had no meaning.

Q&A
Gravity in Space Investigated

Q. What is gravity?

A. A force like a magnet that pulls objects together.

Q. What affects gravity?

A. The size and closeness of objects.

Q. Which planets have the most gravity?

A. Planets with the largest diameters have the most gravity.

Q. What properties do not affect gravity?

A. Atmosphere, temperature, magnetic field, and distance from the Sun do not affect a planet's gravity.

Q. Why are planets in motion?

A. The Sun's gravity pulls the planets in orbit around it.

Q. What is the effect of the Sun's gravity?

A. The closer the planet is to the Sun, the greater the pull and the faster the planet orbits.

Q. Why do objects stay in orbit rather than fall?

A. They are falling as they are being pulled toward the center of gravity. However, they are also traveling at speed (velocity) and the center (i.e. planet or star) curves away beneath the object so it never gets any closer.

Q. Why do astronauts appear to float in space?

A. Gravity pulls everything at the same speed, whatever the size. So the spacecraft, the crew, and the objects are all falling together.

Q. Is there zero gravity in space?

A. No, gravity is everywhere. Gravity never disappears but it may just get weaker at some points.

Q. What causes gravity?

A. Unknown. . .

Objects in Space

One of the major hazards in the solar system are the pieces of space rock, metal, and dust of various sizes, whizzing around.

METEOROIDS

Small chunks of rock and metal that travel through space. They differ in size and can range from tiny grains to over 3 feet (1 m) wide. They are often propelled through Earth's atmosphere at great speed, where they will burn up as soon as they hit the air. This produces streaks of light across the sky that people often call shooting stars.

ASTEROIDS

Like meteoroids, asteroids are made of rock and metal. However, they are much larger and can reach lengths of up to hundreds of miles. They are thought to have been created by rubble left over from the formation of planets. Most asteroids are found in the asteroid belt between Mars and Jupiter.

COMETS
The structure of a comet is comprised of rock, dust, ice, and frozen gases. When comets pass close to the Sun, their surface evaporates because of the extreme heat, releasing gas and dust that get blown into a tail behind them. The body of a comet can measure between 1 and 50 miles (80 km) wide but its tail can reach tens of millions of miles long.

METEORITES
When meteoroids have entered the Earth's atmosphere and come to rest on the surface, they are called meteorites. Most meteoroids don't make it to this stage as they burn to dust upon entering our atmosphere.

COSMIC DUST
Less like the dust that you are likely to find on Earth but more similar to smoke, cosmic dust is made up of tiny particles that float around in space. They range in size from just a few microscopic molecules to grains measuring 0.1 mm. Dust is formed in stars and is then blown away by star explosions. Cosmic dust can then help form the basis for the growth of new stars.

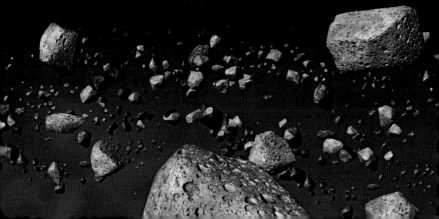

Famous Space Films

The mystery and thrill of space exploration has captured our imaginations in the movies.

1902: A Trip to the Moon (Le Voyage dans de Lune)
Director: Georges Méliès

In this French silent film, a group of astronomers is fired to the Moon in a cannon-propelled spaceship to explore its surface.

1968: 2001: A Space Odyssey
Director: Stanley Kubrick

After finding a strange black pillar on the Moon, a group of scientists embark on a space mission to discover where it came from. However, tensions rise when their onboard computer starts to turn against them.

1950: Destination Moon
Director: Irving Pichel

This was one of the first space films to attempt to include a high level of accurate scientific detail. Four astronauts successfully land on the Moon but realize that they may not have enough fuel left for their journey back to Earth.

1979: Star Trek: The Motion Picture
Director: Robert Wise

This was the first film based on the *Star Trek* television series. Set in the future 23rd century, the film follows the crew of the spaceship *USS Enterprise* as they try to save the Earth from destruction.

2008: Wall-E
Director: Andrew Stanton

In the distant future, humans have had to abandon the huge garbage dump that Earth has become and move to live on a spaceship. A small robot called Wall-E stays behind on Earth to try and clean up the mess, until he meets fellow robot EVE and realizes that life is still possible on the planet.

1995: Apollo 13
Director: Ron Howard

Based on the true story of the 1970 Apollo 13 lunar mission crisis, NASA's third lunar landing is threatened after an oxygen tank explodes on board the spaceship. The crew are in danger of running out of oxygen and not being able to reenter the Earth's atmosphere. They seek help from Houston's NASA mission control, making "Houston, we have a problem" one of the most famous phrases in film history.

Chapter 7

Landing

"Casper! Hirohito! Lucy! Maria! Wake up!" Rachel was walking around the cabin, shaking their shoulders. "It's OK. We're in planetary orbit. We're safe."

One by one, they shook themselves, and unbuckled their harnesses.

"I've got a terrible headache!" moaned Casper.

Jude was already sitting by the viewport, gazing out.

"Look!" he pointed. "Beautiful... there is an ocean... and green land."

Hirohito joined him. "Wow! I want to go down there."

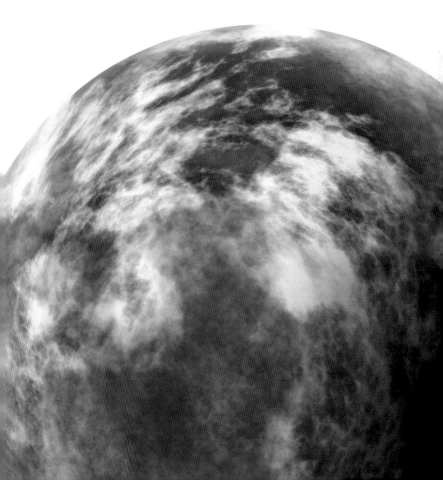

Lucy elbowed the two guys away from the viewport so she could see too.

"Yeah, and get some fresh air!" She took a deep breath. "Not like this recycled stuff we've all inhaled a million times."

"Actually, more like three point one million times, Lucy," said Jude. "On average, we take twelve breaths a minute, and we've been…"

"Oh be quiet, Jude. You know what I mean."

They were all crammed around the viewport now, and Hirohito asked the question that had been on all their minds.

"So who's going to stay behind? We were planning to leave a crew of two in orbit when we made the descent."

"I'm not staying!" said Lucy.

"Me neither!" Casper added.

"Just wait, guys. We can all go," Maria butted in. "Jason isn't with us.

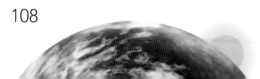

There are five seats on the shuttle. We can leave Rachel in orbit."

The android nodded, "I don't mind doing that."

"Well, let's go, then!" exclaimed Casper, who was already on his way to the airlock where the shuttle lander craft was docked. He punched the panel next to it, and a gentle hiss began. "It should be pressurized by the time we're ready."

It took them an hour to struggle into their suits, helping one another. They tugged themselves through the cramped airlock before putting on their bulky helmets.

"These suits smell!" said Hirohito, as he closed the airlock behind them. "We should have given them an airing."

Rachel's voice crackled over the audio link, "You're confirmed to descend now, team *Argo*! Don't take any risks."

Lucy set the descent controls to automatic and sat back. The craft separated from *Argo* with a low "Clonk." It drifted a safe distance before the thrusters ignited.

It was a routine descent. Lucy took over manual control when they had broken through the cloud-base, and she searched for somewhere to land.

"There's a flat spot over there," said Casper, pointing.

Lucy circled cautiously around. Casper had identified what looked like level grassland not far from the foot of a cliff.

She piloted the craft skillfully into a low glide. "I'm going to try to land.

Hold onto your seats!" She then applied the retro-jets.

When the altimeter showed 30 feet, she tapped in some lift to soften the landing.

"Kicking up some dust!" she said, and then added, triumphantly, "CONTACT!"

Even as they were cheering and taking off their helmets, Maria was checking the sensors.

"Hey!" she exclaimed with delight. "The atmosphere is one-fifth oxygen and four-fifths nitrogen. Now that's real fresh air. Moving, too. There's a strong wind out there."

"What about the biology?" asked Lucy.

"Looking just as good," answered Maria. "This green stuff on the ground contains chlorophyll, so I guess we have to call it plant life."

"Any creatures?"

"Negative on the infrared, so no warm-blooded animals. Just to be on the safe side, we'll stay in our suits. I don't know about you, but I just can't wait any longer. I'm hitting the hatch latch!"

As the door opened, everyone took a deep breath. The fresh air smelled delicious to them, having been without it for 43 long weeks. The retractable steps had barely touched the ground before they were all out of the shuttle and running.

"Oh wow!" Maria shouted. "This must have been what Earth was like before humans… before we…"

"Trashed it?" suggested Hirohito.

"Hey! Wait! One for the photo album," yelled Lucy, and they all swung around and headed back to the shuttle. She perched her camera on a fin of the craft.

"Say cheese!" They all grinned.

"Fromage," said Maria.

"Seriously, guys," Casper called out as they split up. "We don't know what's out there, so we need to be careful. But we should do some serious science. We are the first humans ever to get here. We must take samples of the vegetation, and of the soil and water."

"From the top of that hill, we would have a great view of the surrounding area," said Jude, pointing.

"Why don't you get up there, and do a pano?" Lucy tossed him the camera, and Jude sprinted off. Casper handed out sample bags, and they fanned out around the landing site.

As they collected samples, the wind gradually picked up. It came in gusts, and eventually blew their bags so hard that they had to stop working.

Back at the craft, Lucy scanned the horizon. "Where's Jude? He should be back by now."

She found a pair of binoculars, and trained them on the hill he had run to. It didn't take her long to pick out the blond-haired figure, making his way through vegetation near the summit.

"It looks windy up there," she observed as she watched the figure.

Then suddenly, she dropped
the binoculars…

"NO!"

"What, Lucy? What's happened?"

As she darted for the steps, Lucy
blurted out, "He's fallen! He stood up at
the top of the cliff to wave… the wind…
Give me the emergency kit… I'm going."

She grabbed the red bag quickly
and disappeared.

"Wait, Lucy! We're right behind you!"

It took them ten minutes to reach the
foot of the cliff. They had to fight their
way through thorn bushes that ripped
at their suits and scratched their faces.

Lucy got there first.

Even from a distance, she could see
Jude was badly injured. He was lying
absolutely still on the rock at the foot
of the cliff.

As she drew closer, Lucy sensed that
there was something else very wrong.

Jude's body was lying in a strange, crumpled pose. Lucy had expected to see blood, but there wasn't any. There was a sour smell, like burning plastic.

Only when she stood with Jude right at her feet did she realize the truth. Poking through his torn suit were pieces of shattered carbon fiber and bent titanium.

As the others caught up with her,

panting, Lucy just said, "He was an android."

Maria gasped.

Hirohito spun around adding, "And we have left another android in command of *Argo*."

Maria looked up from the broken body on the ground. "That explains a lot." She stared at her three companions suspiciously. "How can we be sure… that Jude was the only one?"

Hirohito's Space Blog

Earth 2.0 Day 1

Konnichiwa *(Hello)*

There is life outside our solar system! Today I discovered what breathing in unpolluted, clear, fresh air really felt like. Pure, cool, and refreshing, almost sweet to taste as I took deep breaths to fill my lungs completely.

Stepping off the shuttle craft was an exhilarating moment. There was a warm breeze that made the lush green grass rustle as the blades brushed each other. The branches of the trees swayed and the leaves danced high above our heads. There was such variety of different types of plants, many that were unknown to us. The colors of the open flowers were radiant, and the most unusual insects buzzed among them. My fingers tingled with excitement as I touched the soft petals and the smooth leaves. The crisp stems oozed with moist juices traveling up to nourish the leaves.

Everywhere we looked, seedlings were breaking through the rich, dark soil. We could hear the sound of rippling water in bubbling streams. In the distance, we heard strange but happy sounds of creatures calling to each other. This planet is brimming with life. We have so much to study, and learn and discover. We have found a new Eden and this will be our home.

Kangei *(Welcome)*

A Habitable Planet

For life to be possible on planets, certain conditions have to be just right. Too much or not enough of these aspects makes life impossible. In our solar system, only Earth has all the right conditions, but we continue to ask: are there other habitable planets in other star systems?

Temperature

This needs to be in a range of 5°F (-15°C) to 239°F (115°C), so that water can still exist as a liquid. This also allows chemicals needed for life to react together.

Water

This needs to be available so that chemicals for growth and energy can be transported from cell to cell.

Atmosphere

A sufficient gravity that can hold an atmosphere—approximately 100 miles (161 km) thick—is needed to keep the surface warm by trapping heat. Also, it protects the planet from harmful radiation, shields the planet from small- to medium-sized meteorites, and provides gases needed for life, such as nitrogen, oxygen, and carbon dioxide.

Light and chemical energy

Living things use these to run their life processes. There needs to be a steady supply of light at the right temperature and energy-rich chemicals, such as iron and sulfur.

Nutrients

Chemicals are used to build and maintain life. Planets with a water cycle and volcanic activity can circulate and renew the chemicals required.

Galactic Mission Quiz

See if you can remember the answers to these questions about what you have read.

1. What is planet Earth like in 2098?

2. What constellation is Alpha Centauri in?

3. How does the team reach Space Bace?

4. Who was left behind on Space Bace?

5. At what g-force does a typical person lose consciousness?

6. Why are plants such as lentils and herbs chosen for growing on the spacecraft *Argo*?

7. What is the main purpose of a space suit?

8. Name three products that were first used in space?

9. What instructions did Casper use to command Rachel?

10. Who was the first person in space?

11. Why did the team only have one chance of getting into Earth 2.0's orbit?

12. What is the purpose of a planetary slingshot?

13. What is the difference between a meteoroid and a meteorite?

14. Why did the air smell delicious on Earth 2.0?

15. Did the author provide any clues that Jude was an android?

Answers on page 125.

Glossary

Agrisphere
An environment created for growing plants.

Altimeter
An instrument that measures the height of an object above the ground.

Artificial
A copy of something natural made by humans.

Atmosphere
The layer of gases surrounding a planet or star.

Centrifuge
Very fast rotation, or circular movement, around a fixed central point.

Console
The central control panel for communicating and operating between other computers.

Diagnostics
Tests to find data and errors in a computer system.

Elevate
Raise or lift something to a higher position.

Hostile
Not friendly.

Hydroponic
Growth of plants without soil.

Manual
A device or book giving instructions or information.

Microgravity
Very weak gravity, causing near-weightlessness.

Navigator
A person who steers and decides on the direction of a ship or aircraft.

Nutrients
Food or other substances that provide energy and keeps good health for growth.

Pressurized
Put a gas or liquid under a greater pressing force than normal.

Propulsion
Forcefully moving something forward.

Regulation
The rules for keeping people under control.

Relativity drive
The system of moving a spacecraft in time and space.

Retractable
Draw or take back.

Spectrograph
A device for picking up wavelengths of light to identify natural objects.

Synthesized
Sound made electronically.

Trajectory
Flying path of an object through space.

Answers to the Galactic Mission Quiz:
1. Overcrowded with scarce food, water, and land;
2. Centaurus; **3.** By the space tether; **4.** Jason; **5.** 5 g-force;
6. These plants provide a plentiful crop in small spaces;
7. To provide life support in hostile conditions; **8.** *Answers vary from pages 54-55*; **9.** Rachel, listen very carefully; **10.** Yuri Gagarin;
11. *Argo* was low on fuel; **12.** To achieve high speed and change direction by saving fuel; **13.** A meteorite enters the Earth's atmosphere and lands on the surface, but a meteoroid burns up;
14. The students had been used to stale air on the *Argo* and the air was fresher than on Earth; **15.** Jude did not pass out when the others did—*other answers may vary.*

Index

About the Author

Richard Platt was 16 years old when he and his family huddled around a small black-and-white TV to watch Neil Armstrong taking humankind's first steps on the Moon. Richard immediately wanted a job as an astronaut, but gave up the idea when he discovered there were 25 million other children in line, but only three vacancies. He just settled instead for just writing about space—and about technology, history, and dozens of other subjects. In all, Richard has written nearly 100 books for children and adults. When he is not at his desk typing, you'll find him climbing rocks, mending clocks, making bread, fiddling with some computer code, or gardening with his wife Mary.

About the Consultant

Dr. Linda Gambrell, Distinguished Professor of Education at Clemson University, has served as President of the National Reading Conference, the College Reading Association, and the International Reading Association. She is also reading consultant to the *DK Readers*.

Here are some other
DK Adventures you might enjoy.

Terrors of the Deep
Marine biologists Dom and Jake take their deep-sea
submersible down into the world's deepest, darkest
ocean trench, the Mariana Trench.

Horse Club
Emma is so excited—she is going to
horseback-riding camp with her older sister!

In the Shadow of the Volcano
Volcanologist Rosa Carelli and her son Carlo are caught up in
the dramatic events unfolding as Mount Vesuvius re-awakens.

Clash of the Gladiators
Travel back in time to ancient Rome, when gladiators
entertained the crowds. Will they be spared death?

Ballet Academy
Lucy follows her dream as she trains to be a professional
dancer at the Academy. Will she make it through?

The Mummy's Curse
Are our intrepid time travelers cursed? Experience ancient
Egyptian life along the banks of the Nile with them.

Twister: A Terrifying Tale of Superstorms
Jeremy joins his cousins in Tornado Alley for the vacation.
To his surprise, he discovers they are storm chasers, and
has the ride of his life!